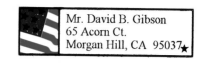

W9-CQV-481

Travel Snapshots
GERMANY

Text
Luisa Tschabushnig

Graphic design
Patrizia Balocco

Contents

Mythical places and historical memories..*page 40*
The smile of a tenacious people............*page 72*
The blending of past and future ....*page 88*

2-3 *The imposing façade of the Altes Museum, built in Berlin in 1824-28 by the architect Schinkel, recalls the classic lines of a Greek temple.*

4-5 *Night lights illuminate Frankfurt, where ancient buildings exist beside modern skyscrapers in an alternation of past and present.*

6 *An interlacing of roads leads to the old town centre of Heidelberg, where Renaissance buildings, museums, and the famous university are situated.*

7 *Prominent features of Heidelberg's landscape are the bridge over the Neckar River and the Church of the Holy Spirit.*

8-9 *Music and good spirits are the most important ingredients of the famous Oktoberfest in Munich.*

10-11 *The wide bight of the Moselle River creates an enchanting landscape between the Rhineland and Lower Palatinate.*

12-13 *The town of Garmisch, a renowned ski resort, is set amongst the Wetterstein mountains.*

14-15 *The land of Bavaria is extraordinarily rich in wonderful buildings and noble residences.*

16-17 *The snowcapped peaks of the Allgau Alps tower over the village of Oberstdorf.*

Published in North America by
AAA Publishing
1000 AAA Drive
Heathrow, Florida 32746
www.aaa.com

© 1992 White Star S.r.l.
Via Candido Sassone, 22/24
13100 Vercelli, Italy
www.whitestar.it

ISBN 1-56251-807-0
1 2 3 4 5 6 06 05 04 03 02

Printed in Singapore
Color separations by Magenta Lit. Con., Singapore

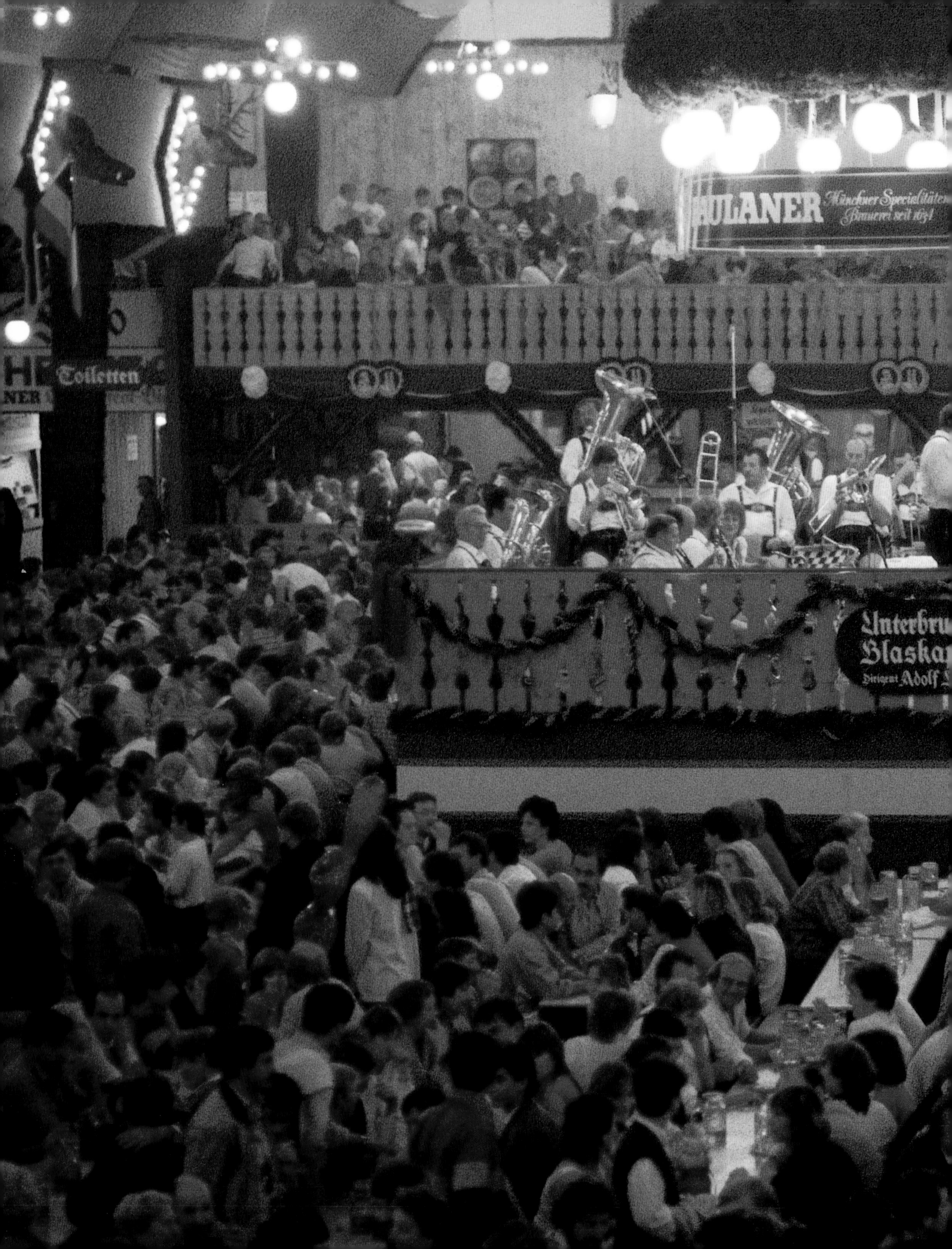
Toiletten

Introduction

Countless different elements shape the character of a country, and many of those elements are continuously changing. On one side, the geographical configuration — the so-called physical geography of a territory — defines one aspect of a country, but the relationship that exists between man and his land down through the centuries is the main force that shapes the spirit of a nation. The appearance of Germany reflects step by step the stages in its history. Both the cities and the natural landscapes provide a continuous example of German historical heritage and of a culture that is deeply rooted in its native soil. The most beautiful, artistic, and noble qualities of German civilization come from its 2,000-year-old history. As cathedrals and abbeys, cities and universities were built, the deep love for all aspects of human knowledge that is characteristic of the German spirit began to consolidate, little by little, around them. This nation, which exhibits an endless strength, has been the country of warriors, sovereigns, monks, artists, philosophers, and scientists. Luther, Ludwig II, Goethe, Schiller, Nietzsche, Kant, Bach, Beethoven, Wagner, Freud, Hesse, and Brecht are among the many noteworthy contributors to German culture; a rich parade of extraordinary sensibilities and genial gifts gave life to a vital German world that became known for artistic achievement. Moreover, German art — from the architecture of Gropius and the paintings of Kirchner to avant-garde cinematography — has left in every era indelible traces of the creativity of this nation and its people. If it is true that music and poetry represent the most inner and spontaneous aspect of a people's culture, we could not help but employ as our guides the likes of Beethoven or Schumann, Goethe or Schiller to lead our way to the discovery of Germany.

The awesomeness of this landscape — hardened by icy gorges or softened by boundless green valleys alternating with rivers and woods — undoubtedly stimulated the fancy of the first inhabitants. In fact, they created a series of legends that are enchanting narrations about the origins of Germany. In this fog-wrapped country, the fantastic played an important role; nature and war marked the life of the ancient

Germans, and myths peopled their imaginations with gods, demigods, warriors, holy swords, bountiful trees, and enchanted springs. So Odin, the god of strength and fury, and the Valkyries, virgins who selected the warriors who were to die in the battle, were born. The wonderful beauty of the German landscape, with its often savage and primordial appearance, matches well with the German mythological heritage, and some vistas would have you believe that the magic protagonists of fairy tales and legends really existed, or rather, they still seem to hover in these enchanting places.

It is necessary to start from this natural aspect to understand the inner tension, the dramatic intensity, and the enthusiasm of this undeniably romantic country. Our *Bildung* — our education in the German environment — may be influenced by unknown strengths of nature that are able to evoke both idyllic and infernal atmospheres, mysterious creatures, ghosts, elves, and fairies — all elements of an eternal poetry. Two thousand years ago, the German and Roman civilizations were the main contributors to the shape of European history; their encounters and struggles, relationships and exchanges were important reciprocal influences for the Western world. The oldest records of German populations date back to Pitea of Marseille, who, in the middle of the fourth century B.C., pressed forward to the Northern European seas. Later, starting with Caesar in the second century B.C., various attempts to conquer the country were more or less successful throughout the period of the Empire. The Germans, Thuringians, Bavarians, Saxons, Slavs, and other German tribes living in different areas of the country received a definitive political and territorial structure with the assertion of the Franks' rule. When Charlemagne was crowned emperor in Rome on Christmas Day in 800, a German dynasty joined for the first time under one throne the whole of Western Christendom and at the same time dominated the most glorious political institution of all time — the Holy Roman Empire. In 843, the division of Charlemagne's empire into two kingdoms — the western one, over Roman peoples, and the eastern one, over German peoples — marked the beginning of the history of Germany as an individual political entity. The imperial crown was then handed down to German sovereigns. For three centuries — from Conrad I's to Frederick II's reign — Saxon, Frank, and Swabian emperors succeeded in ruling over the complex feudal framework of the empire. They fought against dukes and princes of the inner regions and even against the papacy and the Italian city-states. The Holy Roman Empire was a

political, religious, and social institution that infused the German spirit during the Middle Ages with a deep sense of civilization. An identical spirit moved the knights of the powerful Teutonic order to fully "Germanize" the territories east of the Elbe.

In 1250, after Frederick II's death, the apparatus of the empire and the image of the Emperor himself showed signs of decline. The Empire was too large to be monitored, so German cities gained greater autonomy, not only in legal and executive power but also in religious, political, and economic arenas. The different cities, made rich by trade, formed alliances, such as the Hanseatic League and the Rhine cities league, to defend their freedom and privileges. During the reign of Charles V, the Protestant reformation, promoted by Luther, exploded on the scene. It quickly garnered followers and spread far and wide, compromising the unity of the Empire. Numerous princes espoused Lutheranism, rebelling against the Emperor, champion of Catholic orthodoxy. The Peace of Augsburg (1555) put an end to the conflict and ratified the subdivision of the empire between the two professed creeds.

The Thirty Years' War, which involved all of Europe, was caused by religious and political problems that had been neglected for ages. A new peace treaty, signed in Westphalia in 1648, put an end to this ruinous war, which left Germany ravaged and impoverished both financially and in terms of population. Depriving the Emperor of his power led to greater self-government for the German states, above all for Bavaria and, even more so, for Prussia, thanks to its sovereign, Frederick II. In a few years, he succeeded in strengthening his armed forces until they became dominant among European countries. If the French Revolution and Napoleon's victories caused the end of the Holy Roman Empire, in 1806, Prussia itself became the symbol of resistance against Napoleon, culminating in the victorious battle of Leipzig, which was the beginning of the end for France.

In 1815, the Congress of Vienna ratified the birth of a German Confederation made up of thirty-eight states, each with autonomy in its home affairs. In the meantime, Prussia, skillfully managed by Bismarck, asserted its will. In 1871, Bismarck, in a masterful display of force and diplomacy, became the first German Chancellor. The rule of Emperor Wilhelm II propelled Germany onto the scene of international politics, encouraging extraordinary economic growth. But German economic politics, spread throughout the world, stood in direct conflict with the economic affairs of the great European powers and led eventually to the First World War. At the end of the conflict, the spirit of revenge revived very quickly, finding its champion in Adolf Hitler's Nazism. In 1945, when the Second World War ended and the Third Reich had been defeated, the Allies occupied Germany, dividing it into two states. In 1961, a wall was built to divide Berlin into two parts, preventing flight from the eastern to the western side. Suddenly, in 1989, when the wall seemed to symbolize the people's souls, Germany again wrote history with its own hand and destroyed the wall. October 3, 1990, the date of German political union, is engraved on people's memories all over the world as the birth of a new era.

The vital energy and the renewing strength of this country often seem to be contained in the sober and austere beauty of its landscape. A silver mountain range is barely visible behind a soft blanket of mist, its peaks seeming to merge into the grey and blue of the sky. The gentle downward slopes of the hills hold stretches of vineyards, while the boundless green meadows below alternate with ponds and cornfields. Tiny villages and farms scattered here and there provide colourful notes in the country. Tall bell towers stand out from the reddish mass of roofs: like protective deities, they watch over life in the narrow lanes and market places, in the shops, and even in the vegetable gardens. Railroad tracks and highways are far away — distant from the edge of the peaceful wood that offers safe shelter for hares, fallow deer, and wild cats. A soft wake breaks the calm of the river as heavy cargo boats glide silently along through the water. It is well known that the presence of a river has a determining effect on a territory, but for the river Rhine something more can be perceived — an exceptional atmosphere that draws its mysterious charm from the past.

The close, indissoluble bond between land and water and the mythical and historical relation between man and river over the centuries have generated a truly "idyllic Rhine." The Rhine is set like a precious stone between the Black Forest and the Vosges Mountains. Imposing and smooth, the river clears its way alongside castles and cathedrals, towns and terraced vineyards. At dawn and at dusk, the ruins of towers and fortresses, wrapped in magic plays of light, seem to emerge from a wonderland. Each spring, thousands of tourists crowd the Rhine on scheduled tours. The quaint wine villages are literally invaded by the colourful crowd noisily taking in the picturesque medieval sites or resting under the pergolas outside the inns, sipping a glass of Riesling to the sound of a band. But the romantic elements of the idyllic Rhine are to be found far from the tour itineraries, in the quiet paths winding along the vineyards, away from the busy banks, in the hidden

18 Bavarian castles, because of their fantastic architecture and romantic background, are among the most fascinating attractions in the region.

19 top The castle of Glückburg, built in the sixteenth century, is surrounded by the Schlossteich, or moat, which reflects its brilliant white walls. The castle is near the city of Flensburg, just a few miles from the Danish border.

19 bottom The Benedictine abbey of Ettal, built in baroque style in the eighteenth century, stands in the green frame of the Bavarian countryside.

meanders of the river, which becomes more and more mysterious. The charm of this river landscape did not go unacknowledged; it influenced all the poets and writers of German Romanticism, including Arnim, Brentano, and Goethe.

The Rhine Valley, aside from being considered a "garden of nature," has assumed the additional significance of a national monument — stronghold of the symbols of German history. Actually, the valley has been, in the past, a border land, a battlefield, and a travel zone. Romans, Germans, Huns, Cossacks, and American soldiers left the traces of their passage and settlements. The city of Mainz is less than 200 kilometers from Cologne, but more than 600 castles and countless Gothic towers and cathedrals dominate the stretch of valley between them. Roman ruins and medieval fortresses, sumptuous baroque façades and romantic castles along the banks of the Rhine played important roles in the making of Europe. The protagonist of a German epic introduces us to this historical and mythological itinerary; it is the statue of Hagen throwing the treasure of the Nibelungs into the Rhine. The statue stands on the banks of the Rhine in Worms.

Along the river stands the Roman Magontiacum, the present-day Mainz; perhaps the best example of a Rhine city, it is quiet and rich in history. In addition to the romantic and splendid cathedrals, there are numerous monuments and museums and a great university dedicated to Johannes Gutenberg. A short distance away, the remains of Charlemagne's royal palace can be found. But the most distinctive element of the landscape from Mainz to Cologne is the vineyard. It is meaningful that a small town near Koblenz is called Bacharach, "altar of Bacchus," because of the boundless rows of vines around it. In similar places, legend may sometimes spring from nature and vice versa. This is the case of the rocks known as the Seven Sisters or the Seven Virgins, which rise suddenly from the waters of the river. Seven young girls were turned into stone by an irrevocable spell — all except Lorelei, who was condemned to bewitch the sailors from a cliff. The legend, celebrated in verse by Brentano and Heine, seems to originate from this magic scenery studded with six wonderful castles. And, on the long winter evenings, some of the old boatmen are ready to swear they have heard the fair Lorelei's song.

The land at the point where the Moselle flows into the Rhine is called Deutsches Eck, "German corner." It is in this picturesque and striking place that the magnificent monument dedicated to William I once

20-21 *In spite of the bombs of the Second World War, Rothenburg has kept its ancient urban structure intact; it is composed of fortifications and towers dating back to the 14th century, of 18th-century gates, and of buildings in the Gothic style.*

stood. During World War II, a grenade completely destroyed the statue of the Emperor, and now only the base remains. In this particular place, where the two rivers meet, and nature, because of the wonderful landscape, can be described in a lyrical way, Koblenz stands proud and stately. In ancient times it was called Confluentia because of its geographic position, and now it enjoys the magnificence of its past through the valuable artistic vestiges it preserves. The artistic treasures introducing us to the past of the town are not only kept in the museums but they also exist in three Romanesque-style churches. St. Castor, St. Florin, and the beautiful Liebfrauenkirche are all examples of Rhine Romanesque architecture. The flow of the Moselle hides many charming views; in its valley is also one of the oldest German towns — Trier. It dates back to the Roman colonization, as witnessed by the famous Nigra Gate, the biggest Roman gate still entirely preserved.

Returning to our imaginary journey along the Rhine, we suddenly realize that the natural scene changes its appearance. The landscape widens and becomes flat, the phantasmagoric rocks and the hills covered with vineyards disappear along the way and are replaced by vast grazing lands and small rural villages. Life passes slowly, without any entertainment, and is marked only by the growing cycles of the fields; the fast rhythm of the city seems miles away, but it is actually possible to see Bonn's lights from the monastery in Waldenberg.

Bonn, with its bright and refined squares and charming paved streets flanked with neoclassic palaces, is quiet and calm. The lovely small shops, especially the wonderful confectioners' shops that appeal to the appetite, and the cozy environment entice the visitor to stay. One must not be deceived by the appearance of this modern city, enormously developed on the left bank of the Rhine; Bonn goes back to the 16th century, when it became the residence of Cologne's Electors, a role it held until 1815. In 1989, the capital celebrated its birthday — 2,000 years after its founding — and among the numerous works of art, the Romanesque Münster Cathedral, built on the foundations of a third-century Roman cemetery, stands out, stately and imposing. Along the northern edge of town stands the house where, on 17 December 1770, Ludwig Van Beethoven was born. The Beethoven House is now a national museum. With such auspicious beginnings, the love for music inevitably developed with extraordinary vitality. Most European students would love to attend Bonn's academy of music in order to improve their skills under the guidance of prestigious and well-known teachers. Every year, Bonn pays homage to its

renowned son through a major international festival, the Beethovenfest, where concerts, shows, and seminars, all dedicated to Beethoven's works, follow one another. However, music is deeply felt throughout Germany; every town, from the biggest to the smallest, has at least one concert hall, if not an opera house.

In the opera houses of Berlin, Hamburg, Cologne, Stuttgart, and Munich, which were built according to the most sophisticated acoustic techniques, one sees performances of operas taken from both traditional and modern repertoires, and costumes and avant-garde stage designs are often employed for the first time. In addition to the operas, the symphonic network offers a wide range of orchestral groups that are known and admired all over the world. Among them are the Berlin Philharmonic Orchestra, the Bamberg Symphonic Orchestra, and the Munich and Frankfurt Orchestras. The passion for commemorative celebrations prompted several towns to organize a musical festival dedicated to a composer who was born or lived in the town. Ausbach pays homage to its genius, Johann Sebastian Bach, and Bayreuth celebrates Richard Wagner.

As we continue our tour along the Rhine, the river banks become less steep and the landscape more solitary and quiet. Then, suddenly, Cologne appears in all its magnificence. For 2,000 years, the splendid Rhine capital has been the glorious "gate" of this river. Stretching before us, beautiful and self-confident, is a powerful city where history and progress have mingled to create an extraordinary dynamism and harmony. The old streets, with their unmistakable character, guide us through places where, on one side, Roman ruins, medieval monuments, 16th-century buildings, and baroque palaces mingle, and on the other, numerous bell towers, rising towards the sky, stand beside modern skyscrapers. During the magnificent Roman Empire, Cologne was the capital of all of Lower Germany. In the medieval period, it gained the name of "the holy city." In fact, the spiritual life of the city was enriched by the presence of famous theologians such as Albertus Magnus and Eckhart. Distinctive among the monasteries and churches is the extraordinary Gothic cathedral. The Cathedral is Cologne itself; its mass is so mighty and infinite that, together with its spires, it overlooks the whole city. The foundation on which the cathedral stands was once the location of a Roman temple dedicated to Mercury and then of a Carolingian cathedral. In 1164, the removal of the Magi's relics from Milan to Cologne, ordered by Barbarossa (Frederick I), prompted the people to build a more stately cathedral in the Gothic style. Cologne is known as the upholder of the brightest and truest German spirit; this prominence, and the famous Carnival, contributed to its being nicknamed the "town of sin." The vitality of Cologne's inhabitants is shown in its liveliest aspect during the Carnival, which is officially declared on 11 November at 11:11 p.m. The Carnival then begins at the end of January with the election of the Carnival Prince. Masked balls and pageants follow one another without end; among them, the most extraordinary, attracting more than two million spectators each year, is the Rosenmontagzug, where hundreds of allegorical wagons and thousands of costumed citizens join in the parade.

Today, the old German spirit seems to be revived in Düsseldorf more than anywhere else. It is one of the main centres of the Ruhr industrial basin and a remarkable river port, thanks to its position on the Rhine. The city is a magnet for the commercial and financial activities not only of the valley but of the entire country. Deeply damaged by the war, Düsseldorf was rebuilt from a magnificent plan that turned it into a sparkling and futuristic town, interested in the American market and ready to absorb all the first signs of the new Europe. Düsseldorf loves being abreast of fashion, and the style of its nights compares with Paris or London; smart shops and advertising agencies mingle with offices and banks along the Königsallee, or "KO," as the inhabitants lovingly call it. The main street ends in a luxuriant park, the Hofgarten, a green curtain opening on the town centre. The wide park surrounds the sumptuous Schloss Jagerhof, a magnificent 18th-century building.

Heidelberg lies not far from the Rhine plain on the banks of the Neckar, another river dear to the Germans, and is surrounded by striking, wooded mountains. In 1386, the prestigious university, considered to be the cradle of German Romanticism, was founded.

The landscape of Lower Saxony is remarkable for its wild appearance. The wide northern plains extend as far as the eye can see, and the Harz Mountains rise above the cold banks of the Leine. The biting wind blows in from the North Sea, dispersing the fog from the river and suddenly revealing woods, villages, and small cities scattered in the plain. Here more than anywhere else, the climate and the cycle of the seasons call for different rhythms of life, more limited to inner boundaries and to cozy, intimate environments. Even though the damage caused by World War II seriously compromised the artistic heritage of many towns, numerous interesting and beautiful buildings tenaciously survived. The hearts of these towns contain unexpected oases of art and history, and the towns themselves have

been rebuilt according to modern plans.

A case in point is Hanover, where the narrow houses, mainly of wood, complement the Gothic style that here represents the dominant motif of the old historic centre. The old Market Church and the old Town Hall are excellent examples, with their wonderful, well-preserved façades of terracotta tiles, of the high artistic range achieved by the skilled northern builders. The philosopher Leibniz, who lived in Hanover during the second half of the 17th century, described this town as the liveliest intellectual and artistic centre of Germany. In the same period, Princess Sophia commissioned a marvellous castle and garden to be built here. The work was given to Venetian architect Gerolamo Sartorio, but today, only prints and oil paintings reproduce the extreme refinements of the building. The wonderful French gardens are preserved, however, and reveal, through grottoes, waterfalls, small lakes, labyrinths, and an open-air theatre, an intricate and unexpected baroque style within the more severe structure of the city.

The presence of rivers enables the inhabitants of this region to create on their banks the main spheres of activity. Today, they turn their attention to industries of international importance. The lakes and watercourses have often become lines of communication; the Mittellandkanal is a focal point for all German river trade. An enormous number of ships and large barges fill the waters, while a dark smoke spews forth from rusty shipyards and docking platforms, making the edges of the landscape hazy, as in an impressionist painting. Although this scenery does not hold a particular charm, it represents an aspect of Germany that is difficult to ignore. This is a very regular and industrious world peopled by workers, who, along the banks of the Mittellandkanal and in the Ruhr basin, in the Saarland or in the big industrial cities of Cologne and Kassel, keep German industrial production active.

Following the course of the Weser River, we arrive in Bremen, a historic industrial town founded by Charlemagne. Bremen is the second most important German port — a true commercial pole. The intense activity marking the life of this town is a result of the presence of a great number of industries. As you arrive in the Markplatz, you experience the sensation of returning to the past. A marvellous expanse of buildings, culminating in the Gothic cathedral, fills the visitor's view. Among the many structures, the town hall façade, famous throughout Germany and commonly known as "the Weser's Renaissance masterpiece," is especially prominent. Various statues greet the visitor to the old city of Bremen; they are neither generals nor kings, but imaginary and legendary personalities that weave a

22 top The four bell towers of the cathedral loom high above the enchanting rooftops of Bamberg. The cathedral was built by order of the emperor Henry II, and was consecrated in 1012; it caught fire twice, and was rebuilt in 1237, as the Romanesque style of architecture was giving way to the Gothic.

22 middle The church and monastery of Malchon stand on the shores of Lake Medilensburger.

22 bottom The landscape along the Moselle River is marked by green vineyards overlooked by old bell towers and glorious castles.

23 Passau, one of the most beautiful towns in Bavaria, stands at the confluence of the Danube, the Inn, and the Ilz Rivers. In the photograph, one can distinguish the domes of the cathedral, the eastern section of which is late Gothic, while the western section is baroque.

fascinating tale between imagination and reality, romantic belief and history. Roland watches over the middle of the square. A popular Gothic image, Roland protects the town with his legendary sword beside him.

Another renowned statue stands in front of the town hall; it portrays the Bremen Stadtmusikanten — the playing animals of the Grimms' fairy tale. A building covered entirely with glass suddenly diverts us from the medieval atmosphere previously enjoyed; it is the Stock Exchange Palace, a futuristic building that, surprisingly, does not interrupt the architectural harmony. On the contrary, it seems to have been planned to provide mirrors in which the old buildings of the town could be reflected. But perhaps the most genuine feature of Bremen and its inhabitants is hidden in the smoky halls of a few old inns and pubs that have not changed over the years. In places such as the Schnoor and the Dortmunder Union am Dom, time seems to have stood still.

The predominant colours found in this northern landscape are grey, blue, and green; the towns in these areas seem to have the same shades as if nature herself had painted them. In Hamburg, the grey of the fog mixes in with the shapes of the houses and buildings, while light blue waters seem to pervade the whole city. The green grass of the tree-lined roads and the numerous parks attract attention, and they are considered to be "healthy areas" among the neighbourhoods of the metropolis. And what a metropolis it is! Hamburg is a real focal point for the mass media; thanks to nearly 3,000 press offices, Hamburg emerges as the most up-to-date town as far as journalistic tendencies and trends are concerned. You have only to say that twenty-five per cent of newspapers, forty per cent of magazines, and eighty-five per cent of German weeklies have their offices here. Publishing houses, broadcasting stations, record and cinema companies contribute to the town's far-reaching reputation as a leader in the information and communications fields. In 1189, Frederick Barbarossa granted a "distinctive letter" to Hamburg, giving the city a large role in the powerful association of the towns on the North Sea. From there it was titled a "free Hanseatic town," and, after it strengthened its supremacy in the overseas trade, it became a necessary stopover station for wheat, beer, and countless other products bound for the countries overlooking the Baltic and for western Europe.

Hamburg suffered almost total destruction in the Second World War, and about ninety per cent of the port system was lost. However, it succeeded in recovering, thanks to the spirit and temperament of its

24 top *The courses of numerous rivers enliven the calm beauty of Germany. Warm colours and enchanting, almost autumnal, lights are characteristic features of the Middle European landscape.*

24 bottom *The chalk cliffs in Rügen in the Baltic Sea are the most remarkable and famous aspect of the island.*

25 *The so-called "Saxon Swizerland" is marked by a particularly rough and rocky soil. The bridge of Bastel, situated at a dizzying height, and the peaks of Liliensterin create an extraordinary scenario.*

people, who are in some ways very Anglo-Saxon. Here again, an entrepreneurial mentality and a cosmopolitan spirit, acquired as a result of the sea trade, are the beginning elements that lead to wealth and a dynamic lifestyle. In spite of the harsh disparity between the residential neighbourhoods, such as Harvestehude and Poseldorf, and some ill-fated streets near the harbour, the town boasts a great number of multimillionaires. However, neither welfare nor wealth is on display, and a discreet balance between moderation and sobriety exists. Among the old churches, the high bell tower of St. Michaelis (affectionately called "Michael") stands out. The attractive buildings, ranging from the baroque period to Art Nouveau to the modern Chilehaus, show a strong inclination towards architectural solutions that allowed new shapes to blend with the historic aspect of the city.

Northwest of Hamburg, where the North Sea touches Denmark, are the Friesian Islands. The most beautiful of these German islands, in many peoples' opinion, is the Island of Sylt. A wild and unpolluted paradise, Sylt has become a favourite "hideaway" for the wealthy middle-class from Hamburg and Berlin, who have converted the old houses of Friesian fishermen into smart residences for exclusive holidays. On this island, the magic atmosphere described by Thomas Mann in his *Buddenbrooks* lives again — the cries of seagulls soaring over the sea, the rough green waves crashing into the steep, rocky slopes with a continuous, deafening noise.

The absolute power of art enables us to wander freely, without limits or boundaries, and make a geographical leap. Following our route, we reach Travemünde, in Schleswig-Holstein, the northernmost land in Germany. Mann wrote here some of the finest pages of his already mentioned novel. Travemünde, whose name means "mouth of the Trave," is an old village born of the seafaring vocation. Now a fashionable resort, in the past it was a popular meeting place for noblemen and middle-class people from all over Europe. A hundred years ago, the aristocracy mixed seaside activities with gambling here. Today, it is difficult to recapture the atmosphere of Tony Buddenbrooks' carefree holidays among bathers and tourists. Some fleeting images of that period seem to live again under the white arcade of the Kurhaus Hotel. The real Travemünde, made up of boatmen and sailors, is much more difficult to find; a few subtle elements can be discerned in the typical way of speaking called *plattdeutsch*, spoken by the simple people living in the enchanting small houses of Gothmund, a village where the fishing boats can be seen sitting at anchor beyond

26 top *Goethe's native home is in Weimar.*

26 bottom *Prince von Fürstenberg's imposing palace overlooks the waters of the Danube.*

27 top *The New Castle of Meersburg in Baden-Württemberg, an elegant baroque residence, was built by order of the Bishop Princes of Constance in the mid-eighteenth century, on plans by B. Neuman.*

27 bottom *The equestrian statue dedicated to William the Great stands in front of the Imperial Palace in Goslar.*

28-29 *Night lights fall over Deutsches Eck, near Koblenz, at the confluence of the Rhine and Moselle Rivers.*

30 top *In Berlin, modern buildings flank the ruins of the Gedachtinskirche. The buildings were designed by E. Eiermann in 1961.*

30 bottom *The huge complex known as the "red city council" dates back to 1861 and is decorated with thirty-six clay reliefs that tell the history of Berlin.*

31 top *In Berlin, the Reichstag, distinctive for its huge peristyle, was once the seat of Parliament; today it houses exhibitions and displays.*

31 bottom *The Victory Tower is dedicated to the battles of Germany during the age of the Hohenzollerns. Behind it to the left is the Fernsehturm — the television signal tower that overlooks Berlin.*

the small vegetable gardens.

A few miles away is Lübeck, the pearl of the Hanseatic towns. It was founded a thousand years ago, and after two centuries, it became the most flourishing city in the Hanseatic League, which dominated trade across northern Europe. Today, it is still possible to see the brick houses, with their typical steep roofs, whose attics and warehouses once stored goods — salt from Lüneburger Heide, textiles from Flanders, furs from the Ural mountains, vintage wines from Bordeaux, and Scandinavian fish. Over the centuries, the churches of the city were embellished and the civil institutions prospered, thanks to the pragmatic spirit of the city-dwellers who, meanwhile, enjoyed the pleasures of life. The most generous among them founded a series of charitable institutions, providing in their courtyards houses for the poor, still visible and in great demand today as fashionable houses. All the houses in Lübeck have the same architectural quality; they expand towards the inner courtyards because of rigid city regulations that restrict the overall dimensions of the buildings along the road front. The old town centre of Lübeck, proclaimed, in 1987, the "cultural heritage of mankind," is now filled with restoration work that aims to bring hundreds of buildings back to their original magnificence. A remarkable record of the historic warehouses still remains; these are the old salt warehouses, or Salzpeicher, next to Holstentor, a famous symbol of the city. Lübeck is called "the city of the seven towers," for the number of the pointed brick bell towers that fill its sky. Prominent among them are the bell towers of the beloved Marien-kirche, where Thomas Mann was christened. Here also is the Buddenbrookhaus, today a bank, but in the past, the writer's grandfather's house, chosen as the residence for a not-so-imaginary dynasty. A 16th-century façade attracts our attention: it belongs to one of the most representative buildings of the historical Lübeck — the Schiffergesellschaft — once a shipping company, and today, the most famous restaurant in the city. Seated at the 16th-century tables, one can enjoy unique marine specialities, such as Labskaus, a dish of beetroot and dried mackerel and one of the main courses on board ships. All the courses are served with the full-bodied Rotspon, the typical wine of Lübeck. A kind of Bordeaux, it is aged in the cellars of the city, in keeping with an ancient tradition.

Along our trail of the ancient and busy northern cities, we find Kiel, the chief town of the land called Schleswig-Holstein and a seat of important government bodies and renowned scientific institutes. This town, with its strong Scandinavian features, is situated in a wonderful area dotted with lakes, streams, and ponds, amid a landscape that resembles a naif painting. The country is a constellation of ancient rural cottages with thatched roofs; the big windmill of Grebin and the panoramic turret of Hessenstein are two characteristic points of reference in this quiet paradise. In this "region of the five lakes," the farm of Rixdorf, its 17th-century structure still undamaged, is situated among several aristocratic villas — sites for frequent concerts during the summer. On the Panker estate, the Prince of Assia is still breeding racehorses, and in the lovely historic restaurant "Ole Liese," a cozy 18th-century atmosphere will make us lose our way back. Saxony was the true centre of the religious reformation, and still today, one can visit the church door in Wittenberg, where Luther, on 31 October 1517, posted his famous Ninety-Five Theses.

Undoubtedly, this evangelical background influenced the development of political and economic life, but it did not prevent Saxony from becoming, under different circumstances, a battlefield during the religious wars. In spite of these events, several cities experienced intense booming periods, promoting the development of literature and the arts. During his nearly forty years of reign, Augustus "the Strong" changed Dresden, seat of the Electors, into the most beautiful German city of the first half of the 18th century. It was actually his love of beauty and the arts that gave Dresden the name of "Florence on the Elbe." Augustus II made use of skilful architects, both from Germany and from foreign countries. During those years some masterpieces, which are today the wonderful artistic heritage of the city, were created. But it is necessary to point out that the most beautiful images of Dresden live only in the vaporous pastels of 18th-century paintings. In 1945, Dresden was razed after one day and night of continuous bombings. The colossal reconstruction was a true miracle; the city rose again on a grand scale. The luxurious Zwinger palace has been restored to its original rococo style and even the castle boasts its same, smart arcade. In 1985, the Opera reopened. It overlooks the fine Theater-Platz, the centre of musical life of the town. Only the Frauenkirche is still a ruin, in memory of wartime destruction. When sunset falls over Dresden, a magic cone of light illuminates monuments and buildings, gliding over the golden statue of Augustus the Strong and the Albertinum cupola. The Palace of Albertinum houses the rich art collections of which Dresden is so proud. The most important treasure is the Madonna Sistina by Raphael, shown in the Grüne Gewolbe Hall.

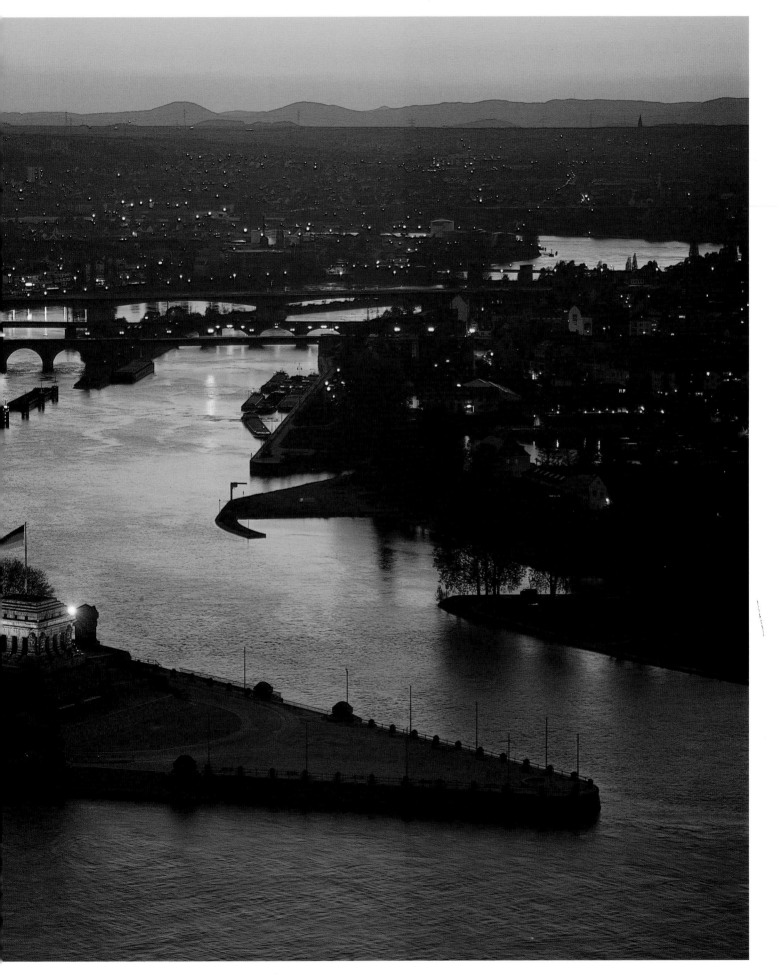

Moving up the Elbe, we reach the so-called "Switzerland in Saxony" — a bright highland beloved by the Saxons. Here, a visit to Leipzig, traditional cultural center of the country, is called for. The beginning of the century marked the greatest growth of the city, which was then, thanks to its fair, an unequalled business center in central Germany. Leipzig obtained, at the same time, its reputation as a famous cultural city, thanks to the prestige of a venerable university, founded in 1409 and attended by Lessing and Nietzsche, among others. Numerous printing works and an important book fair contributed to strengthen the city's image as a literary capital.

Going on our way, we reach Berlin, a city unique in the world and the heart of the country. The shadow of history here was so cruel as to transform itself into an all-powerful barrier against which the bravest and the most rebellious wills could do nothing. Berlin is a human and inhuman city. It is sweet in the most romantic of recollections and honest and ardent in the east borough, which today fades into an aching memory. Berlin has always been dripping with a vital energy that made it able to live with the wall — to fight it, to paint it with the colors of a denied freedom, and finally, to annihilate it in an unforgettable moment of flags and tears. Berlin is healing. For all these reasons and for many others, most private, Berlin lingers in the hearts of those who visit it. In 1949, the planting of a lime tree on the terrace of the Grosser Stern inside the Tiergarten, an 18th-century park completely destroyed by the war, symbolized a return to life for the city and the start of the rebuilding. The lime tree would seem to be the green thread that runs through Berlin. Unter den Linden, the promenade of lime trees, was first traced in 1647, and in 1737, Frederick the Great made it an urban masterpiece.

The post-war rebuilding brought the most fashionable street of Berlin back to its former elegance. The huge avenue is 200 feet wide and continues for a mile from the Brandenburg gate. The modern answer to this monument of absolute elegance and Prussian grandiosity is the Kurfursterndamm, the main street of Berlin, heart of the economic life of the metropolis. The best-known hotels, theaters, cinemas, shops, fashionable clubs, and the most modern libraries are set along this thoroughfare, where life moves at a frenzied pace at all hours of the day and night.

A main junction of local traffic is the Breitscheidplatz, from which the main streets of the city radiate, among these the Kurfursterndamm. The square is towered over by the Kaiser-Wilhelm Gedachtniskirche, which became the symbol of the city

after the war. The clock of the neo-Gothic tower was switched on, and every hour it plays a melody composed by Prince Ludwig Ferdinand of Hohenzollern. On the side of the ruins are two buildings constructed by Eiermann in 1961. The Berliners call the big octagonal chapel and the hexagonal tower "compact" and "lipstick," respectively. Behind the church, the skyscraper called the Europa Center rises up. It holds commercial businesses, international clubs, and nightclubs. The "isle of the museums" is one of the most famous little museum towns in the world. The vastness of the collections and the great value of the treasures accumulated here form a real "town" of art and historical documents.

The history of Germany still lives intensely in the wide region which once was known as Swabia. At present, this region is no longer part of the political and territorial German entity. Rather, it represents a historical memory, a national symbol of the ancient power of the German aristocracy. The duchy of Swabia extended from the Asperg hills north of Stuttgart to the Alpine passes which now belong to Switzerland. The crests of noble Swabian families, such as Hohenstaufen and Hohenzollern, appeared alongside the imperial crest very often. Barbarossa and Frederick II belonged to these illustrious families, as did Konrad of Swabia, whose death caused the noble dynasty to be extinguished. Swabia, which had been the heart of the Holy Roman Empire and the whole of Germany for two centuries, broke up into several territories and colonies, losing all political authority. Princes, knights, and clerics took possession of one section and tried to enrich their own territories in every field. For this reason, within a geographically narrow area, one can find numerous castles and extraordinarily artistic monasteries — beautiful representations of the German baroque style. The castle of Sigmaringen, wonderfully situated on the Danube, and the splendid monasteries of Roggenburg, Ottobeuren, and Weingarten, with the biggest baroque dome north of the Alps, are just a few of the major monuments of Swabia.

In the southern part of the Jura of Swabia flows the Danube, born of the Black Forest. The river has opened up a beautiful valley flanked by rocks and medieval villages. Here the real spirit of the old Swabian people still lives. These people belong to an ethnic group which still today is united by a particular local dialect, a derivation of the old Alemannic. It is not always easy to trace the Swabian roots, since this region quickly opened itself up to progress, favoring industry and the development of services. Some very famous inventors and industrialists worked in this land, among them Robert Bosch, and Gottlieb Daimler, who invented the first gasoline, self-igniting engine at the end of last century and wrote the birth certificate of the German motor industry.

Far away from the industrial areas, the architectural structure of some towns proves how time has not always made strong changes. This is so in the case of Tübingen, where nice wood houses face the river Neckar; these are the houses of the students' quarters, where renowned guests such as Kepler, Hegel, Schelling, Hilferding, and Hesse once lived. Today, Tübingen is still the most famous German university, preserving its 15th-century Gothic charm unchanged.

In towns such as Ulm, Regensburg, and Reutlingen, life goes on in an almost 19th-century rhythm. Renaissance bell towers and huge domes resembling bulbs tower over the reddish mass of the roofs. That is the way the sky of Augsburg appears. It is a city rich in 16th-century façades, prestigious symbols, and reminders of the political leadership played in the era of Charles V and the Fuggers, a powerful family of bankers. It is not accidental that a renowned tourist itinerary among these towns is called the "Romantic Road."

At the time of the political and territorial shattering of Swabia, the Earls of Württemberg were more successful than any others in the garnering of land; they conquered a wide region around Stuttgart. Today, the hinterland of Stuttgart is an economical pole of the federal region of the Baden-Württemberg and is one of the largest areas of industrial concentration in Germany.

Despite the mark of progress in its most avant-garde forms, the balance with the architectural styles of the past does not seem disturbed. The medieval atmospheres are unchanged, along with the equally romantic ones the 19th century left in large quantity — the two spectacular baroque castles in Stuttgart and Ludwigsburg, for example. Travelling towards Nuremberg through a countryside which slopes down into the woods, one has the feeling of having already stepped into Bavaria, as no sign delineates the Franconian frontier. Franconia belongs to Bavaria, not for historical or cultural reasons, but political ones. This territorial arrangement was ratified by a treaty signed by Napoleon to indemnify the loss of the Bavarian territories on the left side of the Rhine. In Nuremberg, it is impossible not to be caught up in the silence and the medieval calm which reign here. All the pride of this population is contained in the severe and dark sandstone bulk of the Gothic Lorenzkirche. Not far from the church and the Museum Bridge, one can admire one of the most beautiful views of the

town in the quiet cove of the Pegnitz, near the old hospital. On summer nights in the streets of Nuremberg, life is intense; people stay late in the pubs, chatting and sipping the local beer, which is as dark as coffee.

If you want to discover the real atmosphere of old Germany, you have to turn to Bamberg. On walking through the narrow streets flanked by fishermen's and craftsmen's simple houses painted in lively colours, you will reach the majestic historical centre where the cathedral and the extraordinary palace of the archbishop rise up. If, instead, you are interested in the archetype of the German woods, you have to follow the way to the mountains and the thick forests east of Bayreuth. The Fichtelgebirge, with its wonderful trees and strange stones, is the place of origin of many sagas and fairy tales. Fairy tales are often close to mind as we discover Germany and the deepest German spirit, but they are not considered a fleeting escape from reality so much as an interpretation of nature and her power.

To understand thoroughly this romantic attitude towards the fantastic, the castles of Bavaria are necessary stops. The German castle is everywhere the symbol of aristocracy, artistic patronage, and beauty. The castles that King Ludwig built have an irresistible charm. A worthy example of this charm is the Castle of Neuschwanstein, with its immaculate towers and its dark blue pinnacles. All your fantastic dreams can be realized here. It is as if a spell has been cast over these places, causing everyone who visits to lose every link with reality. The world seems to have awakened from a long sleep in an atmosphere where everything is possible and where the sky and the forest seem brighter than anywhere else.

In Munich, one has the happy and reassuring sensation of being at one's own home, where people are received in a warm, friendly atmosphere of freedom, open to fun as well as to art and culture. If it is not superior to other towns in the number and importance of its monuments, it is certainly the greatest for its concentration of museums and artistic collections, cultural shows, and music festivals. Culture has its own temples at the renowned University and in the Academy of Art and Music. The non-stop activity of this cosmopolitan town does not deprive it of its carefree and lively aspect, renewed, at every season, by happy and popular festivals. Munich is famous all over the world for these traditional annual celebrations. These grand parties last several days, and they eventually turn into colossal *kermesses*, where huge quantities of meat and sausage are consumed, together with oceans of beer, of which Munich is the uncontested capital. The two most important and spectacular festivals are the Oktoberfest and the Carnival. The Oktoberfest lasts a fortnight between the end of September and the beginning of October and was first observed in 1810. It takes place on the Theresienwiese, among fairground stalls and attractions of every kind, to the sound of folk orchestras. The Carnival is the most spectacular in all of Germany, assembling allegorical carts and folk groups from every part of the region.

Speaking of prestigious and lively towns, the refined Frankfurt plays an important role as a financial and commercial capital. It is the site of numerous fairs, the most famous of which is the Book Fair, known all over the world. The origins of this town date back to 794, when it was the seat of one of Charlemagne's imperial palaces. In 1330, it was allowed to celebrate yearly the Festenmesse, the Lenten fair which had been considered the most important in Europe for centuries. In 1866 the annexation to the King of Prussia marked the peak of the economic activity of Frankfurt, thanks also to the banking activity carried out by the renowned Rothschild family. The present character of Germany shows a strongly competitive nation which has maintained and strengthened the economic vitality of its past along with a passion for art and scientific research — projecting itself as a major player on the international scene.

Mythical places
and historical memories

Perhaps the most admired monuments in southern Germany are the castles of Ludwig II of Bavaria: the summer residence of Linderhof in Oberammergau — a tiny treasure in the rococo style; the castle of Herrenchiemsee, built on an islet of the homonymous lake after the style of the Palace of Versailles; and the castle of Neuschwanstein near Füssen.

The royal castle of Hohenschwangau had its first period of splendour during the 12th century as the centre of the minnesingers — German lyric poets and singers. The knights of Schwangau died out in the 16th century, and the castle went to ruin until 1832, when it was bought by Crown Prince Maximiliam II, Ludwig's father.

40 top *The magnificent castle in Herrenchiemsee, modelled after Versailles, has a façade rich in details. Part of the palace has been transformed into a museum devoted to Ludwig II, King of Bavaria.*

40 bottom *The castle of Hohenschwangau was built in neo-Gothic style in 1833-37 by Maximilian of Bavaria.*

41 *The wonderful castle of Linderhof, built in 1870-74 for King Ludwig II of Bavaria, combines Renaissance stylistic elements with typical baroque.*

At King Ludwig's court

When riding, King Ludwig often visited a particularly fascinating place not far from the ancient Hohenschwangau castle. On Schwanstein, a hill of the Tegelsberg range, are the ruins of a fortress. The old castle walls can still be identified, as some are still rising toward the sky. The reconstruction work commissioned by the king in 1868

lasted seventeen years and restored the main structure of the fabulous Neuschwanstein castle, as fascinating as it is sadly famous. It is here that Ludwig II spent the last days of his tormented life. The castle's internal hallways are lined with fine oak timber. The paintings depict legends and mythological themes of Wagnerian inspiration. The lamps and the intricate steel trim, the curtains and the tapestries are decorated with pictures of elegant swans, and their shape and variety bear witness to the excellent workmanship of the artisans employed by the romantic sovereign.

The magic ring of the Bavarian Alps

44 *The small towns of the Bavarian Alps are known for a particular decorative style; the fronts of the houses, especially the most ancient ones, are frescoed with floral patterns and graceful ornaments and have reflected the faith and devotion of the inhabitants throughout the centuries.*

Bayer. Volkskunst
J. Sorge

82

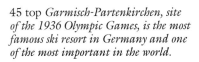

45 top *Garmisch-Partenkirchen, site of the 1936 Olympic Games, is the most famous ski resort in Germany and one of the most important in the world.*

45 bottom *Stucco and sculpture, brass and wrought iron enrich even the most sober Bavarian house fronts.*

46-47 *The cold waters of alpine lakes and rivers often become permanent residences for entire colonies of swans. This photograph shows a pleasant winter scene in Füssen.*

The journey through the Bavarian Alps is mainly reserved for lovers of mountain terrain. Covering the entire length of the famous Deutsche Alpenstrasse, one reaches the wonderful stretch joining Tegernsee to Berchtesgaden. Majestic mountains and peaks reaching bravely for the sky, narrow and deep valleys crisscrossed by

foaming streams, and dense woods and crystal clear lakes form the extraordinary alpine landscape. Picturesque villages are brought to life by numerous skiers and climbers who find, particularly in the central massif area, excellent facilities.

48 *A gauzy haze of clouds covers the city of Berchtesgaden, one of the most handsome vacation resorts and health spas in the Bavarian Alps.*

48-49 *The solemn Wetterstein range is dotted by the Alpspitze peaks of the Waxenstein and by the Zugspitze "pyramid."*

The German landscape is dominated by woods, which cover more than twenty-eight per cent of the country's land surface. The north Atlantic region contains hardwood forests and heath, distinguished by holly and ash, while the central and southern region is covered by magnificent beeches and red and white fir trees. Roebucks, chamois, marmots, and fallow deer constitute most of the German fauna, now carefully protected in numerous national parks and reserves.

52-53 Winters are long and often snowy; from the blank white cover urban centres rise suddenly, and roads and tracks trace surreal patterns.

A fairy-tale atmosphere

The "Romantische Strasse" is Germany's most famous tourist itinerary. It runs completely through Bavarian land and, beyond Augsburg, into the so-called "Bavarian Swabia." The scenery is varied and evocative: first, low hills introduce you to the vast Lechfeld plain; then, the

landscape comes alive — the hills are more pronounced and are covered with pine and oak forests; finally, you reach the narrow Tauber Valley, home of the famous Swabian vineyards. Here the towns of Augusta, Dinkelsbühl, Rothenburg, and Würzburg boast medieval art treasures and sumptuous baroque buildings.

54 *Lake Constance offers glimpses of evocative landscapes; emerging from the green of the enchanting natural picture is man's sober architecture, such as the ancient Meersburg castle.*

55 *The route that stretches from Füssen to Würzburg through Augsburg and Rothenburg is called the "Romantische Strasse" for the dreamy beauty springing from the towns and for the fairy-tale buildings that one encounters along the road. In this picture is the Kapuzinerpath at Dinkelsbühl in Bavaria.*

56-57 *At Dinkelsbühl — a delightful medieval village surrounded by ancient turreted walls — balconies and window sills "bloom" with cascades of variegated geraniums.*

The valley of Father Rhine

The Rhine offers a scenic/historical itinerary among the most evocative and popular in Europe. The stretch joining Koblenz to Mainz travels past more than 600 castles, pleasant expanses of vineyards, and ancient towns. The peak of fascination is reached at the sumptuous Deutsches Eck — the confluence of the Rhine and the Moselle Rivers. Towards Bonn, the scenery becomes calmer, and the waters appear to be almost a prelude to the Nordic Sea.

58 Fable and reality come together in the magic scenery of the Rhine Valley; on an islet in the middle of the river stands the Pfalzgrafenstein Castle, built by the Emperor Ludwig IV in 1327.

59 top The journey along the Rhine moves from wonder to wonder; the emerald green of the vineyards that cover the hills is interrupted by the walls and pinnacles of fortresses and abbeys. In this view, one can make out the Castle of Stableck.

59 bottom Bacharach is a picturesque wine village, where typical latticed houses are gathered around the market square and the ancient parish.

The quiet
stillness of the fields

Thanks to intensive mechanized cultivation, Germany can satisfy most of its food needs through the very high yields of its crops. The main agricultural products are cereal grains, potatoes, and sugar beet. Of particular local importance is the cultivation of grapevines along the Rhine and the Moselle and in the

Palatinate. A considerable contribution to the German agricultural economy is made by forestry, which annually produces a large quantity of timber. The countryside offers picturesque and evocative perspectives, where the charm of the old farming tradition is recaptured in the characteristic architecture of the ancient farms.

60 *The wooded slopes of the Black Forest hide quiet farming villages, where time is still marked by the changing of seasons and the tilling of the fields.*

61 *The colours of the impending autumn lend a golden appearance to the countryside and the work of ploughing.*

Imprints
of civilization
unaltered
by time

62 top *The Porta Nigra at Trier, built during the second half of the fourth century, was surmounted in 1041 by a church in honor of the monk Simeon. Napoleon had the church demolished and the illustrious monument restored to its imperial grandeur.*

62 bottom *Autumn colors mix well with the rose color of the Mespelbrunn residence in Franconia. The castle, silently mirrored in a pond, was partially rebuilt in 1564 in the style of the Renaissance; it still belongs to the Count of Ingelheim.*

63 *St. Peter's Cathedral, in Worms — a renowned Roman Palatinate set on the left bank of the Rhine — is one of the most important Romanesque monuments in all of Germany. The earliest structure was built by order of the Holy Roman Emperor Henry II, beginning in 1018, while the current structure was begun in 1171.*

64-65 *Among the many castles and royal palaces in Germany, the Swerin and Rheinsburg castles are two of the most evocative. These architectural structures blend harmoniously with the natural surroundings.*

The north wind

Schleswig-Holstein, the land in extreme northern Germany, occupies the base of the Jutland peninsula between the Danish border, the Schwerin Strait, and Lower Saxony. The west coast is characterized by peat bogs and swamps, while the eastern one, on the Baltic Sea, offers an open and fertile countryside interspersed with lakes. Connected with the many ports on the North Sea are the wild Friesian Islands, the remains of an ancient coastline destroyed by marine eruptions. The natural scenery of these islands is absolutely unique; alongside sandy and rocky beaches stretches a healthy expanse of meadows and tilled fields.

66 Odd combinations enliven the landscape in the Nordic region. As if in a painting, a coloured lighthouse overlooks a field of sunflowers on Fehmarn Island.

67 The Schleswig-Holstein countryside is strewn with picturesque mills, some of which are very ancient, like the one at Farve, built in 1828.

68 *The glow of sunset lends an evocative and mysterious appearance to the little island of Helgoland, located in the North Sea, 43 miles from the Elba estuary.*

69 *Helgoland Island presents a varied and diversified scenery; eroded, rocky cliffs alternate with inhabited areas, divided into two parts — Unterland and Oberland — while the area to the north is an agricultural reserve.*

The skies over the Friesian Islands

The sky in the north country reflects a beauty that is absolutely indescribable. The play of winds makes for an extreme variability of clouds that follow the changing mood of the scenery, where the colours of blue and ash mix in a thousand subtle shades. All Germany knows the fascination of skies scarcely lit by the sun, penetrated by bell towers and the roof peaks of houses,

or filled with blue above the waterways. But it is here, in the extreme north islands, where the urban presence is diminished and the beauty of German scenery explodes in all its natural charm. The Eastern Friesians lie between the mouths of the Ems and Weser rivers. The Northern Friesians are located just off the western coast of Schleswig.

The smile of
a tenacious people

Munich is a pleasant and welcoming town. The wide and busy streets, the gardens, the small restaurants, and the honest and open style of the architecture all inspire a feeling of warmth and friendliness. In addition, Munich embodies the convivial spirit and happiness typical of Bavarians. Drinking a good tankard of beer has become something of a ritual, and beer halls, open day and night, represent a favourite meeting place for celebration or casual conversation. To understand how deeply rooted these traditions are, one must only consider that the Hofbrauhaus — the most famous beer hall in Munich, visited every year by millions of people — dates back to 1589.

72 top *The Oktoberfest is not to be missed by those who wish to sample the true taste of one of the most popular celebrations in the world. Good cheer and filled tankards reign for fifteen days, and under the multicoloured pavilions one can meet people of every nationality.*

72 bottom *Music is an essential part of the atmosphere at the Hofbrauhaus; the evening is spent merrily, well into the early hours, between singing and abundant food. The habitués, who keep their own personal tankards at the beer hall, drink alongside visitors from all over the world.*

73 *Every year, the Oktoberfest transforms the urban landscape of Munich and fosters a euphoric spirit among the inhabitants. The Theresienwiese is filled with festive pavilions of every kind.*

The impeccable city

Financial business, like every other German market activity, is concentrated in the stock exchange building in Frankfurt. Along with Wall Street, Milan, London, and Tokyo, Frankfurt is an important international financial centre. The high concentration of business going on in the stock exchange is related to industrial and commercial enterprises across the nation, to the stock companies, and to the public banks. These activities are important elements of the German economic world, all of them daily converging in Frankfurt. Some of the typical characteristics of modern stock exchange transactions date back to exchange operations of the Middle Ages, when merchants and salesmen of free German towns cultivated commercial connections with Holland, Flanders, and northern Europe through the Frankfurt Trade Fair.

74 The Frankfurt Stock Exchange is a prominent centre of activity in the international financial world.

74-75 The role of active financial and commercial capital city played by Frankfurt is shown above all in the bold and futuristic style of its buildings. The Dresdner Bank, a skyscraper of glass and steel, is a clear example.

Man's work . . .
a mirror of the times

76 *A craftsman at work in the celebrated porcelain factory in Fürstenberg, founded in 1747. The city, which stands by the Weser River, also houses a Porcelain Museum which contains some remarkable masterpieces.*

76-77 *Germany is essentially an industrial country that derives its energy mainly from mining resources — in particular, the coal deposits of the Ruhr and Saar areas.*

An uncommon island life

The archipelago of the Eastern Friesian Islands includes seven small islands arranged in a crescent just above the northern coastline. These low, sandy lands, continuously altered by the mighty winds of the

North Sea, consist of long stretches of wide beaches. New, rapidly growing seaside resorts have replaced maritime activities. The people are still tenaciously bound to their own dialect and to the Calvinist religion.

78-79 *Both the Eastern Friesians and the northern archipelago boast modern seaside and thermal resorts. The beaches are characterized by "hampers," which allow the occupant to relax on the beach, sheltered from the sun and wind.*

Popular traditions and the joy of life

Masked parades, frequent occurrences during Carnival, which is mainly celebrated in the Rhineland, Baden-Württemberg, and Bavaria, allow the German people to give shape to their imaginations, often with grotesque or baroque "characters." The fortnight consecrated to Carnival undoubtedly represents a recovery of

legendary and fairy-like images from the ancestral patrimony of German culture. A veritable army of witches, fairies, elves, and gnomes overruns the streets of towns and villages; the presence of costumes inspired by superhuman figures is related to the cult of nature and its invisible forces, inherited from the ancient popular traditions still alive in peasant civilization.

80-81 *The Cologne carnival is one of the most famous in Germany; the women's Shrove Thursday procession takes place in the Alter Markt Square.*

81 *In picturesque Urach Square in Baden-Württemberg, children dressed in typical folkloric costumes celebrate the carnival with a dance.*

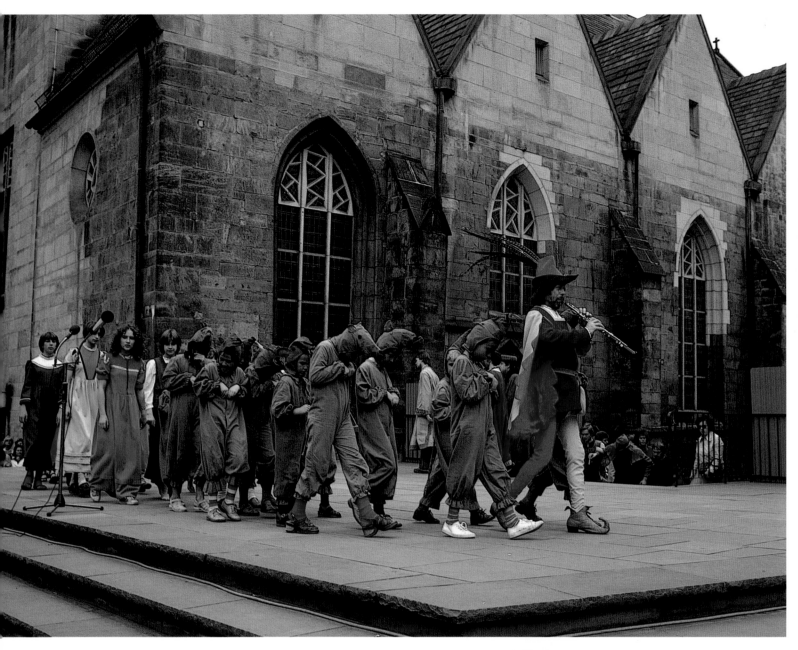

82 top *The beautiful town of Hameln in Lower Saxony is pleasantly renowned; popular tradition refers to it as the setting of the tale of the Pied Piper, immortalized in the fable of "The Magic Flute" and celebrated every year with a whimsical parade.*

82 bottom *From the 15th to the 24th of July, the town of Dinkelsbühl, a delightful medieval town in Bavaria, commemorates its anniversary with historical floats, popular dancing, and costume parades.*

83 *A festive parade featuring women in their costumes riding a painted cart takes place in the small town of Bad Tölz, a major thermal spa on the Isar River.*

A typical manifestation of popular handicrafts is clothing. The costumes are often brilliantly coloured; women wear scarlet skirts, complemented by richly detailed blouses and lace scarves. Bonnets and hats vary according to the area — patched along the northern coastline, white in the Palatinate, black in Westphalia, and gold in the southern areas. The traditional male clothing includes a

velvet jacket hemmed with precious embroidery, and the typical hats, with and without plumes. Today, these clothes are worn almost exclusively on the occasion of special historical and religious occasions.

84 *A line of silver buttons and an eccentric hat are often part of German folk costumes.*

84-85 *The odd hat of the Cologne costume requires many hours of work and skill on the part of the artisan.*

The principality in miniature

Bückeburg castle, a jewel of Renaissance architecture, is one of the most representative monuments of the town which was the capital city of the small principality of Schaumburg-Lippe until 1918. Dancing parties and elegant all-night balls are often held in the sumptuous halls of the castle. The magnificent rooms, adorned by ancient mirrors and furniture, provide a bright backdrop for lively dancing and a merry atmosphere. During the celebrations and anniversary festivals, the inhabitants of Bückeburg usually wear elaborate costumes characterized by large, dark bonnets, as tradition in Westphalia requires.

The blending of past and future

Many German towns offer an elegant, harmonious blend of structures of medieval origin and more modern features. The heart of German towns remains the "markt," the ancient market square and theater of the primary public and historical events. The restrained medieval context often remains untouched, overlooked by the rathaus, the town hall, and the cathedral. The other buildings and the true body of the town gather round the market square. Baroque and neo-classical features mingle with 19th-century gardens and modern buildings. The orderly suburban areas are devoted to the large industrial estates.

88 top Kiel, the main German Baltic harbor, situated at the bottom of a wonderful bay (Kieler Forde), is at present the centre of the German naval industry. The close bond between the inhabitants and the sea is especially apparent in June, when the town hosts a colossal regatta — the most important marine festival in Germany.

88 bottom Snow-laden contours emphasize the solid and stately structure of the Würzburg residence, built by Balthasar Neumann in the 17th century.

89 The popular Gothic statue dedicated to the paladin Orlando stands in the center of the main square in Bremen. The glorious hero of the Carolingian epic is portrayed with the sword of justice and a shield with the imperial eagle.

The united city

90 top and bottom *The urban plan for the rebuilding of Berlin after the war availed itself of the experience of some of the most innovative contemporary architects of the day. This enabled the city to assume its present cosmopolitan look. These photographs show some views of contemporary Berlin; glass, steel, cement, and granite are the major elements of the new urban design.*

90-91 *Marx-Engels Bridge links the homonymous square to the Unter den Linden. The bridge, designed by Schinkel, is adorned with eight allegorical statues.*

91 top and bottom *The Berlin Philharmonic Orchestra performs in one of the most traditional and sacred temples of symphonic music.*

92-93 *The triumphal Brandenburg Gate, the symbol of the city, is an imposing, classically-inspired portico, 85 feet high and 204 feet long, built between 1788 and 1791 by Carl Langhaus.*

94 *Breitscheidplatz is the traffic fulcrum in Berlin; it is distinguished by the symbolic monument of the Kaiser Wilhelm Gedachtniskirche. The neo-Gothic tower creates an unusual contrast to the hexagonal building of Eiermann, built during the sixties.*

95 *Charlottenburg Castle, the largest and most famous in Berlin, was built by Arnold Nering in 1695 as a royal country residence. Beyond the castle is the park, designed by French and English architects, where the new pavilion and the Belvedere, a graceful tea house built by Langhaus in 1788, are located.*

Potsdam . . . the baroque plans of Frederick the Great

The town of Potsdam boasts a great number of elegant expressions of late baroque style and neo-classical architecture. The New Palace, the Marble Palace, and Charlottenhof Castle are among them. From the 17th century onwards, it was the permanent residence of the Prussian kings. During this glorious period, it was highly favoured by Frederick the Great, who promoted its artistic and cultural growth. The plans of Sans-Souci castle, characterized by refined rococo interiors and a magnificent park, are the work of the foresighted sovereign. Potsdam is historically famous because of the homonymous conference, when Stalin, Churchill, and Truman met in 1945 at the end of the Second World War.

96 top *Baroque friezes and sculptures enrich the front of Sans-Souci castle, built in Neo-Classical style, with broad windows overlooking the park and friezes that recall the rococo interiors.*

96 middle *The caryatids, which enliven the Neo-Classical lines of San-Souci's façade with their naturalistic stances and poses, were designed and executed by Fr. Ch. Glum and J.A. Nahal.*

96 bottom *A fanciful rococo pavilion is situated in Sans-Souci's stately park.*

96 right *A perfect 18th-century style dominates the princely halls of the New Palace, built by the architects J.G. Büring and H.L. Manger in a classical style with rococo interiors.*

97 *Gold flashes in the ornaments of a "berceau" in Sans-Souci park.*

The ancient heart of the financial capital

Frankfurt appeared for the first time in history in 794 as the seat of one of Charlemagne's royal palaces. After 814, it became the favourite residence of the Carolingian emperors. From 1152 onward, it was the seat of imperial elections, and, from 1562 until the end of the 18th century, of coronations. Its economic ascent began in 1212, when it proclaimed itself a free town. The Fastenmesse, or Lent Fair, celebrated annually since 1330, only increased the city's prestige and wealth. The urban fabric of Frankfurt mirrors the economic aspirations and the historical past of the people. The Romerberg is the main square, the true heart of the city and the scene of coronation ceremonies and of the fair itself.

98 *The Romer is the famous Frankfurt town hall, made up of three buildings: in the middle, the "Zum Romer" house dating back to 1322, on the left, the Alt-Limpurg, and on the right, the Lowenstein.*

99 left *The cathedral tower, one of the most ancient monuments in Frankfurt, reaches to the sky. The structure that we see today, rebuilt after the war, was erected between 1205 and 1269, and the tower, 311 feet tall, was begun in 1415, based on a plan by Maderm Gertheren.*

99 top *Today the ancient parade ground is a lively business centre in the heart of the city. Here the Hauptwache, a guard room in 1730, stands adorned by a triangular pediment bearing the town arms.*

99 right *The Hauptwache café is one of Frankfurt's most renowned meeting places.*

100-101 *The 17th-century Fountain of Justice stands in the centre of the Romerberg.*

102 *One wing of the Frankfurt historical museum shows the destruction of the town during the Second World War, through plastic models, maps, and photographs.*

103 *The charming roofs of the 18th-century houses, characterized by picturesque attics and garrets, lend an an impressive air of glamour to Frankfurt.*

104 top *Schiller's statue stands out against a vitreous background of skyscrapers.*

104 bottom *Eschenheimer Strasse, one of the main highways in Frankfurt, leads from the walls of the ancient ramparts to the heart of the city, crossing the business quarter.*

104 right *A modern building, built according to the latest architectural trends, houses the famous Frankfurt Fair.*

104-105 *The imposing neo-classic façade of the Opera in Frankfurt stands in contrast to a modern building; this scene is typical of the urban appearance of Frankfurt.*

Between the city
and the canals . . .
the charm of Hamburg

106 left *The ancient sections of Hamburg have retained the true and original appearance of a typical Nordic city. In this view, one can see the elegant structures of the old warehouses.*

106 right *This picture shows the venerable buildings of the Potters' Guild.*

106-107 *The inland basins of Alster, in the centre of Hamburg, are charming and distinctive.*

108-109 *The port of Hamburg is one of the most important in the world for shipping traffic. It was founded in the middle of the tenth century, and it has been enlarged repeatedly, until it reached its current dimensions in 1858. The port is about ten miles long and covers a surface of over sixty square miles.*

Munich . . .
the true heart of Bavaria

At the heart of the city, the Marienplatz is the theatre for the most important historical events in Munich. The northern side of the square is taken up by the Neues Rathaus, left, a neo-Gothic building dating back to the end of last century. The most important attraction is the famous carillon, the largest in Germany. Another monument and symbol of the city is magnificent cathedral, the Frauenkirche.

112 top Pictured here are two unmistakable details of Munich — the gold statue of the Virgin, and, in the background, the famous carillon.

112 middle The wonderful palace of Nymphenburg was the summer residence of Bavarian sovereigns until 1918. The duke Ferdinand Maria gave it to his wife, Henrietta of Savoy, as a gift.

112 bottom The Staatsoper, the National Theatre of Opera, is recognizable by its imposing façade.

112-113 The Residenz was the seat of the Bavarian dukes; the Throne Room is a brilliant example of ornamentation, paintings, and 18th- century stuccos.

Stuttgart . . .
the elegance of discretion

Stuttgart is one of the best examples of urban order and elegant architectural arrangement. An enviable town plan, respectful of the environment, and several buildings that represent the heritage of the past, join with the simplicity of the

neoclassical style, framed by green backgrounds that contain the Baroque and Renaissance remains from the destruction of the war. Even modern elements, including new residential quarters and shopping centres, have been woven into the fabric of the city without conflict.

114 *The Altes Schloss, a Renaissance castle, was built by Alberlin Tretsc at the end of the 14th century. The palace is composed of a wonderful courtyard and a chapel, while the Württembergisches Landes museum is situated in the main wing. A vast and charming garden with fountains surrounds the palace.*

115 *Situated within a luxuriant park, a plain building in neoclassic style houses the National Theatre. The presence of wonderful open spaces is a delightful constant in the urban fabric of the city of Stuttgart.*

Dresden . . . details of a noble past

116 *The Clock Pavilion is an integral part of the magnificent Zwinger palace, a princely residence built according to the plans of M. A. Pöppelmann in 1711-1722.*

117 top *The historical past of Dresden can be read on the imposing structure of the Baroque castle of Moritzburg.*

117 bottom *The ancient market square, as seen from the tower of the city hall, is the true heart of the city.*

118-119 *An imposing castle overlooks the wonderful panorama of Heidelberg. It is built on a hill, 328 feet above the city.*

The beauty
of detail

120 top *The cathedral of Freiburg, begun in 1200, is one of the most important Gothic buildings in Germany. Its red limestone framework is crowned by a spectacular octagonal Gothic tower 377 feet tall.*

120 middle *Hanover, a northern city with a vast heritage, boasts numerous museums and art galleries. The picture shows the Leibniz Haus, where the philosopher resided until his death in 1716; Leibniz is buried in the Johanniskirche.*

120 bottom *The enchanting baroque town of Würzburg, in Lower Franconia, is situated among lovely vineyard-rich hills on the left bank of the Main River. Its most splendid age was from 1650 to 1750, when the princes of the Von Schönborn family encouraged the development of the arts. Balthasar Neumann's architecture and Tiepolo's frescoes date back to this period.*

121 *Cheerful shops enliven the main square in Bonn.*

Under a sky of bell towers

122 *In Lübeck, the panorama is distinguished by the presence of several bell towers, especially those of the Marienkirche and Peterskirche. The Marienkirche, begun in 1260 and completed in 1330, is the largest and most handsome Gothic brick church in all of Germany. The Peterkirche, also Gothic, dates from the fourteenth or fifteenth century.*

122 right *In Nuremberg, the main square is known for both its Schoner Brunnen, a famous fountain by a master from Prague, and its town hall.*

123 *From the top of a baroque tower in Leipzig, a historic clock has kept the time since 1556.*

124-125 *The glow of sunset reveals the true charm of Düsseldorf along the river. From 1614, it was the capital city of a palatine principality, and during the postwar period, it was revived as a modern and lively city.*

126-127 *In the old town centre of Cologne, the equestrian monument to Kaiser Wilhelm and the metal frameworks of a modern building frame the spires of the famous cathedral. One of the most spectacular Gothic cathedrals, it stands on the site of an ancient Roman temple dedicated to Mercury. The cathedral, begun in 1248, was built as a shrine to house the relecs of the Three Magi, which were brought to Cologne at the orders of Frederick Barbarossa in 1164. It was inaugurated by the Emperor Wilhelm II in 1880.*

Photo Credits:

Marcello Bertinetti/White Star archives:
Page 1; 4-5; 12-13; 14-15;
36-37; 40 bottom; 43; 44; 45; 46-47; 49;
52-53; 74; 75; 91 top; 96; 97; 98; 99;
100-101; 102; 103; 104; 105; 112 top.
Giulio Veggi/White Star archives:
Pages 2-3; 30; 31; 32 top; 33; 90;
91 bottom; 94; 95; 128.
Antonio Attini/White Star archives:
Pages 10-11; 32 bottom; 72 bottom;
112 bottom; 113.
M.B./Apa Photo Agency: Pages 118-119.
N.Bahmsen/Zefa: Page 82 top.
Reiner Behnke: Pages 24 top, 68.
Rino Bianchi/Shot Photo: Page 26 bottom.
Josip Ciganovic/Shot Photo:
Pages 22 bottom; 41.
Dallas & John Heaton/Apa Photo Agency:
Pages 7; 19 bottom; 40 top; 59; 110; 111;
112 middle.
Damm/Zefa:
Page 28-29; 48; 63; 73; 116; 126-127.
D. Davies/Zefa: Page 62 top.
*Joel Ducange/Figaro Magazine/Grazia
Neri:* Pages 60; 61.
Rob. Everts/Zefa: Page 22 top.
Alain Evrard/Apa Photo Agency:
Page 106 left.
Klaus D. Francke/Bilderberg/Grazia Neri:
Pages 86; 87.
Ralf Freyer: Pages 22 middle; 26 top.
Cesare Gerolimetto: Page 6.
Michael Hilgert/Apa Photo Agency:
Pages 27 top; 54; 55; 56-57; 66; 67;
Kalt/Zefa: Page 72 top.
Kiedrowski/Zefa: Page 76.

Kohlhas/Zefa: Pages 108-109; 114.
WolfGang Korall: Pages 24 bottom; 79.
Peter Kühn: Page 26 top.
Maximilian Küthe: Pages 70; 71; 120
middle.
Karl Jung/Zefa: Page 121.
*Gerd Ludwig/Woodfin Camp &
Associates/Grazia Neri:* Page 19 top.
Hans Madej/Bilderberg/Grazia Neri:
Page 117.
Paul Mahrt: Pages 64; 65; 69; 89.
*Dilip Mehta/Contact Press Images/Grazia
Neri:* Page 78.
W.H. Mueller/Zefa: Page 115.
Oster/Zefa: Page 88 top.
Udo Pellmann: Page 25.
J. Pfaff/Zefa: Page 80.
Thomas Pflaum/Visum/Grazia Neri:
Page 77.
Luciano Ramires: Pages 50-51.
G.P.Reichell/Apa Photo Agency:
Page 106 right.
Rosenfeld/Zefa: Page 81.
Rossenbach/Zefa: Page 122 left.
J. Schliemann/Zefa: Pages 34-35.
Gregor Maria Schmid: Pages 23; 122 right.
R. Schmid/Zefa: Page 83.
Schroeter/Zefa: Pages 16-17.
Lorenzo Sechi/SIE: Page 27 bottom.
Starfoto/Zefa: Pages 8-9; 58.
Wolfgang Steche/Visum/Grazia Neri:
Pages 84; 85.
E. Streichan/Zefa: pages 10-11; 92-
93; 120 bottom; 124-125.
Walter Thierfelder: Pages 18; 24-25; 38-
39; 62 bottom; 88 bottom; 123.
Adina Tovy/Apa Photo Agency:
Pages 20-21; 82 bottom; 107; 120 top.
Weir/Zefa: Page 42.